AT THE AIRPORT

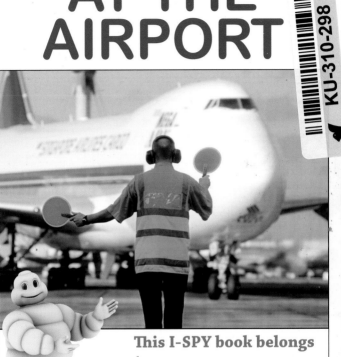

This I-SPY book belongs
to:_____

Introduction

An Airport – especially a busy international one, such as Heathrow – is a very exciting place. People of all nationalities are continuously travelling to and from many different countries around the world. In fact, millions of passengers may pass through an airport every year.

Just imagine how complicated it must be to manage an airport. Firstly, passengers must be able to get to it so that there must be facilities for parking cars for just a few minutes or for perhaps weeks on end. There must be bus stops, taxi ranks, railway stations and even sometimes Underground facilities. When you arrive, you will have to check-in with your chosen airline and your baggage must be handled as well as checked to make sure you are carrying nothing dangerous or illegal. There must be places where you can eat, drink, use toilets, shower, change a baby, or even attend church. There are shops where you can buy all kinds of things from books, magazines and sweets to souvenirs or even clothes. You must be able to find out where to go and what to do so there are information desks and a myriad of signs.

Then you must pass through immigration, where your passport is checked, then on to a further security check before entering the main departure lounge. You will have your hand luggage X-rayed or searched and you may be searched yourself. In the main departure lounge there are more places to eat and drink, as well as more shops. And various kinds of information boards tell you what time your flight is due to depart and from which gate. You may use a moving walkway to take you to your departure gate or there may be an automated Rapid Transit System. Finally, you will board your plane either by a jetty or airbridge, or even by walking across the tarmac, or apron, and up the steps. When you travel, it can be an exciting experience – there is so much to see around you.

You can get even more out of every flight and visit to the airport if you take I-Spy At the Airport with you when you travel.

How to use your I-SPY book

As you work through this book, you will notice that the subjects are arranged in groups which are related to the kinds of places where you are likely to find things. You need 1000 points to send off for your I-Spy certificate (see page 64) but that is not too difficult because there are masses of points in every book. As you make each I-Spy, write your score in the box and, where there is a question, double your score if you can answer it. Check your answer against the correct one on page 63.

To and From the Airport

Airports are usually located where there is enough flat land to allow for one or more level runways to be built as well as the other buildings and structures needed. When new airports are built, the designers also try to keep disturbances to local people to a minimum. Finally, the natural environment must be taken into account. All this means that airports may be some distance from towns or cities, and anyone wishing to travel by air must first be able to get to the airport. There are various ways to approach most airports.

TUBE

You may have travelled to Heathrow Airport by the underground or tube.

Which underground line is Heathrow on?

I-SPY points: 10

Double with answer

Date: _____

TAXI

A taxi is one way to reach the airport...

I-SPY points: 10

Date: _____

TRAIN

...or you may have travelled by train. Many airports have a dedicated train service that takes you to and from the local city centre.

I-SPY points: 10

Date: _____

If you travel by car, it is most likely that you will have parked in one of the long-term car parks.

PARKING ZONE

Remember where you leave your car! Most car parks are very large and it is important to make a note of your parking place

I-SPY points: 10

Date: _____

BUS STOP

You can catch the courtesy bus to the airport terminal from one of the bus stops. Make a note of this stop as it will be the one you need to return to when you collect the car.

I-SPY points: 5

Date: _____

PARKING PAYMENT

Automatic payment machines are located at the car park and often in the airport terminal as well.

I-SPY points: 5

Date: _____

EXPRESS COACH

Express coaches operate between the airport and several other urban centres.

I-SPY points: 10

Date:

LONDON BUS

London buses connect to several stops in Central London.

I-SPY points: 5

Date:

TRANSFER BUS

At a big airport, where there are several terminals, you may need to catch a bus from the long-term car park, or between terminals.

I-SPY points: 5

Date:

PORTER

Whether you arrive by bus, taxi, train or car, you should be able to find a smartly uniformed porter who will, for a fee, take your luggage to the check-in desk.

I-SPY points: 10
Double if you know their nickname

Date: _____

VALET PARKING

Drive to the airport and this service parks your car for you, at a destination away from the airport. When you return from your trip, it will be waiting outside the airport terminal!

I-SPY points: 15

Date: _____

BAGGAGE TROLLEY

You can always use a baggage trolley yourself. Look for these at a trolley park next to the terminal building.

I-SPY points: 5

Date: _____

An airport terminal may offer all kinds of facilities. These can be especially useful if you have had to leave home in a hurry and have forgotten something or if you have time to wait at an airport for a long time.

INFORMATION DESK

Whether you are a passenger or not, you may need to find out the time of a flight or if it has arrived or where you can hire a car. Whatever information you need, the staff at an information desk will try to help.

I-SPY points: 5

Date: _____

TELEPHONE

Calling overseas is an easy task on the phone systems in most airports.

I-SPY points: 10

Date: _____

CHARITY AND DONATIONS

You will find some discreetly positioned charity boxes. All the proceeds given go to very good causes and will accept coins (and notes!) of any currency – a great way to relieve yourself of unwanted foreign currency!

I-SPY points: 10

Date: _____

PHOTO BOOTH

By the time you reach the airport, it's rather late to be getting a passport photograph. On the other hand, they do provide quick and easy photographs.

I-SPY points: 10

Date: _____

POST OFFICE

You can even find a Post Office at the airport – important for buying stamps for that last-minute letter or postcard.

I-SPY points: 10

Date: _____

POST BOX

There is no point in selling stamps if there isn't somewhere to post the letters!

I-SPY points: 10

Date: _____

BUREAU DE CHANGE

At a Bureau de Change you can change money from one currency to another, such as Pounds into US Dollars or Euros.

I-SPY points: 5

Date: _____

BOOK SHOP

Many people buy a book before they fly. It may be a travel guide, a novel or a puzzle book.

Which would you buy?

I-SPY points: 10

Date: _____

SHOPS

Many airports have a collection of designer labels and tax free shopping. Perfect for that gift or present!

I-SPY points: 10

Date: _____

ATM

Cash machines are always available when you need money.

I-SPY points: 5

Date: _____

TV MONITOR

You can catch up to the minute news and events on large TV displays.

I-SPY points: 5

Date: _____

GAMES CENTRE

It is now possible to play some of your favourite electronic games when waiting at an airport.

I-SPY points: 15

Date: _____

RESTAURANT

You might need a snack, or a substantial meal. There are usually a variety of bars, cafes and restaurants at most airports.

I-SPY points: 5 for each of two different kinds

Date:

INTERNET

It's quite easy to keep in touch by e mail or surf the web at one of these special internet stations.

I-SPY points: 10

Date:

KIDS ZONE

Young children can easily get bored waiting at an airport. This especially designed children's lounge is the perfect way to keep occupied.

I-SPY points: 20

<u>Date:</u>

DRINKING FOUNTAIN

Perhaps you're thirsty and just need a drink of water. Signs like this indicate a handy drinking fountain.

I-SPY points: 10

<u>Date:</u>

SECURITY DOG

You won't find one of these sniffer dogs at every airport but they are highly trained to search and find illegal substances.

I-SPY points: 25

<u>Date:</u>

TERMINAL INDICATOR

Large airports have several terminals and you'll need to know from which one your flight departs.

I-SPY points: 10

Date:

TRAVELATOR

You may need to travel by moving walkway...

I-SPY points: 10

Date:

...which have warning signs like these.

I-SPY points: 10

Date:

CONCOURSE

Modern terminal buildings are wonderful structures and the architecture is often overlooked. The picture shows Heathrow's Terminal 5 – the largest free standing structure in the UK.

I-SPY points: 20

Date: _____

TRAIN

To reach your checking-in point you may need to travel on an internal train system.

I-SPY points: 10

Date: _____

COVERED WALKWAY

Have a look where you are walking. If you have to leave one building and travel to another, you may walk along an enclosed bridge connecting the two.

I-SPY points: 20

Date: _____

INFORMATION BOARD

These digital displays are really useful for providing information about your destination. This one shows details about snow conditions at ski resorts.

Have you ever been skiing?

I-SPY points: 15

Date: _____

PRAYER ROOM

Airports are not just about rushing around and catching a flight. You can find these special Prayer Rooms if you need time to reflect and say some prayers.

I-SPY points: 25

Date: _____

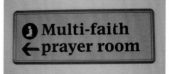

If you are going to travel by air, one of the first things that you will have to do when you arrive at the airport is check-in with the airline that you are travelling with. Usually, dependent on your airline, your destination and the airport, you must do this around two hours before your flight is due to depart. You will need to show your ticket and passport, your luggage will be weighed and checked in and you will be issued with a boarding card. You will also be asked questions concerned with the security of your luggage.

TRAVEL RESTRICTIONS

You will find signs like this in several places around the check-in area. They tell you what you are not allowed to take on board the aircraft and must be obeyed.

I-SPY points: 5

Date: _____

LIQUIDS

Displays like this one show you very clearly exactly what liquids you can and cannot take on board. Only containers of under 100ml are currently allowed in hand luggage.

I-SPY points: 10

Date: _____

HAND LUGGAGE

There is limited space on an aeroplane and you cannot take large bags or packages in the cabin. If your bag can fit into these containers, you may take it on with you.

Where do larger bags and suitcases go?

I-SPY points: 10
Double with answer

Date: _____

CHECK-IN INFORMATION

Large displays tell you where to check in.

I-SPY points: 10

Date: _____

FIRST CLASS

If you are lucky enough to be travelling First or Business Class, you will have your own separate check-in facilities. Some airports also have a Fast Track system for these passengers to board more quickly.

I-SPY points: 15

Date: _____

SELF SERVICE

You can save time by having your tickets issued on the internet and by checking in on the self-service machines. There are always plenty of staff available to help if you need assistance. Here are a selection of check-in machines.

I-SPY points: 10 each

Date: _____

CHECK-IN DESK

If you use the check-in desk, you will be asked a number of security questions, your luggage will be weighed and identification tags put on them. This makes sure that your bags arrive at the same airport as you do, on the same flight!

I-SPY points: 10

Date: _____

OVERSIZED LUGGAGE

Some people have to travel with very large packages or bags. If this is the case, they will be taken to be a special oversized luggage area to be checked in. There may be an excess baggage fee to pay.

I-SPY points: 20

Date: _____

PASSPORT CONTROL

When you are ready and have finished checking-in, you will need to make your way to passport control.

I-SPY points: 10

Date: _____

19

PASSPORT SCAN

Some airports can now check your passport by electronically scanning the details.

I-SPY points: 20

Date: _____

IRIS RECOGNITION

As everyone's eyes are different, Iris recognition a secure way of checking in. Your iris is scanned, and as long as it matches with the image on record, the unmanned immigration barrier opens to allow you through.

I-SPY points: 25

Date: _____

Security is paramount at all airports and you will be required to have your possessions examined and X-rayed, as well as having a body search.

REMOVABLE POSSESSIONS

You will need to put any metal objects, including keys, mobile telephones, money – even belt buckles and shoes into a plastic container that is checked though an X-ray machine.

I-SPY points: 10

Date: _____

X-RAY MACHINE

The X-ray scanner allows bags to be viewed to check their contents. Each item has to be scanned and checked to make sure that it is safe to be allowed on the aeroplane.

I-SPY points: 15

Date: _____

X-RAY OPERATOR

The operators of the machines are skilled technicians who know exactly what to look for when they see the images. If they see anything suspicious, the item will be removed and checked by hand.

I-SPY points: 10

Date: _____

X-RAY IMAGES

By picking up the metal objects as a solid image, any headphones, electronic components, clasps, buckles etc will show up. Anything that is considered dangerous, such as knives, scissors or even knitting needles can be confiscated.

I-SPY points: 20

Date: _____

WALK THROUGH METAL DETECTOR

This is another type of X-ray machine. As you walk through the frame, an alarm is immediately activated if it senses any metal. This could be a belt buckle, keys in a pocket or a watch. You will be asked to remove these items and go through the scanner again.

I-SPY points: 20

Date: _____

Departures

BODY SEARCH

Regardless of the results of the walk through detector, you may also be given a body search. Here a member of security will check your clothes to make sure that nothing is being smuggled on board.

I-SPY points: 15
Double if it happens to you!

Date: _____

HAND HELD WAND

To be certain that you are carrying nothing illegal, and to reinforce the previous searches, you may see a hand-held wand in use. This device is a portable metal detector that can be passed all over the body to be certain that you are not carrying anything illegal.

I-SPY points: 20

Date: _____

DEPARTURE GATE SIGN

Once through security, you will need to look for the sign to the departure gates.

I-SPY points: 10

Date: _____

DEPARTURE GATES

You will need to find the departure gate for your flight. This could mean a long walk or even a journey on an internal train.

I-SPY points: 10

Date: _____

DEPARTURE BOARD

One last check on the departure gate to make sure the flight is on time.

I-SPY points: 5

Date: _____

LOUNGE

You may be lucky enough to be allowed to check in to a private lounge. These are normally only for people travelling first and business class, or by private plane.

I-SPY points: 15
Double if you are allowed in one.

Date: _____

I-SPY points: 15

Date: _____

TRANSIT BUS

Aeroplanes have to park at their designated slot. This may be some way from the departure gate. To arrive there quickly and safely, you may need to travel in a transit bus.

At some airports, you may either have to walk across the apron to board the aircraft or you will be taken in a special bus. As you go, keep a look out on the tarmac: there are all kinds of interesting things to see.

JETTIES

Here is one of the jetties or airbridges that allow passengers to walk straight through from the departure lounge to the door of the aircraft...

I-SPY points: 10

Date: _____

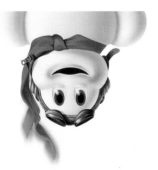

...and here is a jetty being joined to an aircraft.

I-SPY points: 15

Date: _____

Steps were once the most common way to board an aircraft and are still used to board many aircraft, particularly at smaller airports.

The steps in this picture are the most common and you will find these being used to board many aircraft.

I-SPY points: 10

Date:

These enclosed steps make sure that you do not get wet when it is raining!

I-SPY points: 15

Date:

Smaller planes do not need large steps and you may see a truck with steps like the ones in the picture. These are easy to move and can be quickly manoeuvred into position.

I-SPY points: 20

Date:

When you have a meal or a drink on an aeroplane, have you ever stopped to think how the food arrived on board? A catering truck pulls up alongside and when in position, the container is raised by hydraulic lifts until it is level with the opening hatch. The carefully packed food and drink can then be slid along tracks into the hold compartment of the plane.

FREIGHT

A conveyor belt, like this, loads bags and parcels on to an aircraft. It is usually known as a rocket.

I-SPY points: 15

Date: _____

PASSENGERS' BAGGAGE

Passengers' baggage is usually carried to the aircraft in containers on wheeled trollies, called dollies. The containers are known as bins.

I-SPY points: 15

Date: _____

HI-LOADER

Here is another type of freight vehicle – this one is known as a hi-loader.

I-SPY points: 15

Date: _____

TUG

Sometimes, aircraft must be moved in or out of their parking positions by special powerful vehicles, usually called tugs.

I-SPY points: 15, 20 points if you see a tug moving the aircraft

Date: _____

HIGH RISER

This platform allows access to the highest of places!

I-SPY points: 15

Date: _____

HIGH LOADING FREIGHT

Catering bins are lifted up to the hold area of the aeroplane before being rolled into the cargo section.

I-SPY points: 15

Date: _____

I-SPY points: 30

Date: _____

LARGE LOADS

Sometimes aeroplanes have to carry really large loads. Some cargo aeroplanes are specially designed to be able to carry these consignments – if you are lucky you may see one being loaded. Look how the nose section opens up completely.

I-SPY points: 15

Date: _____

BAGGAGE HANDLING

All the suitcases and bags have to be loaded onto the correct aeroplane to make sure that they arrive with you at your destination.

SECURED CONTAINERS

It is important that the contents of any goods that are being loaded are secure and do not fall over or collapse when being moved. Most palletised loads are strapped and secured for loading.

I-SPY points: 20

Date: _____

All aeroplanes need fuel. The aviation fuel is generally taken to the plane so that it can be re-fuelled on the apron. Here are some examples.

POWER TRACK

When an aircraft is on its parking stand, ground power is supplied along one of these power tracks.

I-SPY points: 20

Date: _____

POWER CONNECTION

With the engines shut down, the power is connected to the aircraft. Most stands at busy airports have this type of system.

I-SPY points: 20

Date: _____

FUEL TRUCK

You may see a fuel truck under the wing of an aeroplane with pipes connecting it directly to the fuel tanks.

I-SPY points: 20

Date: _____

POTABLE WATER

As well as re-fuelling, drinking water supplies will also have to be re-filled. Look out for a water truck.

I-SPY points: 25

Date: _____

Here's another type of water truck that you may see.

I-SPY points: 25

Date: _____

I-SPY points: 25

Date: _____

FIRE ENGINE

The emergency services must be ready for any incidents. Test runs are made every day so don't be alarmed if you see them driving around! Fire engines like this one must be at the scene of an accident as quickly as possible.

AMBULANCE

An airport is a very busy place with thousands of people travelling through it every day. Airports can have their own ambulance services which offer assistance to people who fall ill at the airport, as well as to any accidents that may occur from time to time.

I-SPY points: 20

Date: _____

HELICOPTER

You would expect to see aeroplanes at most international airports, but helicopters also fly from many domestic and local ones.

I-SPY points: 20

Date: _____

Here are a few signs that you may see from the aircraft window, or outside the terminal building.

STOP AND LOOK

The many vehicles that work in and around the airport all have to comply with strict traffic controls. This sign indicates that aircraft always have the right of way!

I-SPY points: 20

Date: _____

EMERGENCY SERVICES

In the event of a major incident, it is vital that the emergency services take control of the situation as quickly as possible. You may see an Emergency Services Rendevous Point sign like this one.

I-SPY points: 25

Date: _____

AIRCRAFT VIEWING AREA

Watching or spotting aircraft is a hobby that many people enjoy. Some airports have designated viewing areas, often on the roof or a balcony where you can watch and take pictures of planes landing and taking off.

I-SPY points: 15

Date: _____

SECURITY FENCE

Airports must be secure places and it is vital that no one can enter the airport complex unless they have the correct security clearances and permissions. A tall perimeter fence will encircle most airports.

I-SPY points: 15

Date: _____

WINDSOCK

These strange objects are secured to the top of a post at most airports.

Do you know what they are for?

I-SPY points: 15

Double with answer

Date: _____

RUNWAY AHEAD

You are most likely to see this sign from the aeroplane window just before you take off!

I-SPY points: 15

Date: _____

SECURITY CAMERAS

Security cameras are prominent on both the terminal building and on the runway. This one is aimed at the planes on the apron as they load and unload...

...and this one is close to the runway out in the middle of the airfield.

I-SPY points: 15
for either camera

Date: _____

LANDING LIGHTS

Airfields are well lit at night, on both the sides of the runway, as well as approach markers indicating the beginning of the runway.

I-SPY points: 25

Date: _____

CONTROL TOWER

All flight movements are controlled from the Air Traffic Control Tower. The Control Tower is usually the tallest building at an airport.

Why is the building so tall?

I-SPY points: 15

Double with answer

Date: _____

RADAR

Air Traffic Controllers can monitor the planes on a radar screen. Operators give radio landing instructions to the pilots.

I-SPY points: 10

Date: _____

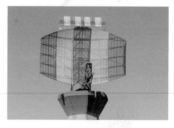

HANGAR

When an aircraft needs maintenance it will be taken to a large hangar. These structures are normally located away from the terminal building.

I-SPY points: 15

Date: _____

CHOCKS

A chock is a sturdy piece of material, placed behind a wheel to prevent accidental movement, when the aircraft is parked.

I-SPY points: 15

Date:

SETS OF WHEELS

A large aeroplane will have many wheels. The tyres on these wheels have to be incredibly strong to withstand the force of landing.

I-SPY points: 25

Date:

COCKPIT

If you are lucky enough, you may see the pilots in the cockpit.

I-SPY points: 20

Date:

TAKE OFF

One of the many sights that you will see at an airport is an aeroplane taking off. You will probably be able to see these from the terminal windows.

How many aeroplanes can you see taking off?

I-SPY points: 10

Date: _____

MOVING AROUND

Ground staff use hand signals to assist the pilot in parking the aeroplane at the correct gate.

I-SPY points: 20

Date: _____

ARRIVALS

When you arrive at your destination, you will need to follow signs for Arrivals. This will take you to the right area for customs clearance and to find your bags and suitcases.

I-SPY points: 10

Date: _____

BAGGAGE RECLAIM

Wherever you have travelled from, you will need to collect your bags before you leave the airport. Look for signs like this one for Baggage Reclaim to retrieve your bags.

I-SPY points: 15

Date: _____

BAGGAGE CAROUSEL

When you reach the arrivals hall, check the notice board to see which baggage carousel your bags will be on. All the bags and suitcases from that flight will be going around, so be sure to double check the bags you take really are yours!

I-SPY points: 15

Date: _____

FLIGHT CONNECTIONS

Not all journeys end when the aeroplane touches down on the runway. You may need to catch another flight to reach your destination. You may see a sign like this one...

I-SPY points: 10

Date: _____

...or one like this, without words.

Why do you think this image has no words on it?

I-SPY points: 20

Double with answer

Date: _____

When you have cleared immigration, and collected your bags you will need to pass through customs. The passage you take will depend on where you have travelled from and what you are carrying.

GREEN CHANNEL

You can go through the green channel if you are travelling from a country outside the European Union, if you are carrying no more that the regular customs allowance and if you are carrying no banned or restricted goods.

I-SPY points: 15

Date: _____

BLUE

Go through the blue channel if you are travelling from a country within the European Union and you have no banned or restricted goods.

I-SPY points: 15

Date: _____

RED

The red channel should be used if you have goods to declare, have commercial goods or if you are not sure which channel to go through.

I-SPY points: 15

Date: _____

UK BORDER

If you are travelling from overseas, you will need to have your passport checked to formally enter the United Kingdom. The immigration officer will do this when your passport is checked at the desk.

I-SPY points: 15

Date:

PERSON WITH SIGN

Some business men and women are collected at the airport, normally by a driver with a car. You will see the drivers holding up a sign with their name, or their company name on it.

I-SPY points: 15

Date:

TOURIST INFORMATION

Once you are through customs, you will probably find a display of information sheets. These may be local maps, tourist information sheets or theatre listings.

I-SPY points: 10

Date:

RESTRICTED ZONE

Many areas within the airport are not open to the general public and you are not allowed to enter them. These places are known as restricted zones.

I-SPY points: 15

Date:

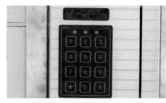

SECURITY KEYPAD

Keypads allow airport staff to pass through secured and locked doors with a special number sequence.

I-SPY points: 15

Date:

INFORMATION SIGN

Here is a list of some of the things that you are not allowed to do at an airport.

I-SPY points: 20

Date:

AER LINGUS
I-SPY points: 10

Date:

AEROFLOT
I-SPY points: 20

Date:

AIR FRANCE
I-SPY points: 10

Date:

AIR INDIA
I-SPY points: 15

Date:

AIR INDIA EXPRESS
I-SPY points: 20

Date:

AIR SEYCHELLES
I-SPY points: 25

Date:

ADRIA AIR SLOVENIA

I-SPY points: 20

Date: _____

AIR SLOVAKIA

I-SPY points: 20

Date: _____

AIR ALGÉRIE

I-SPY points: 20

Date: _____

AIR CANADA
I-SPY points: 10

Date: _____

AIR MALTA
I-SPY points: 15

Date: _____

AIR WALES
I-SPY points: 30

Date: _____

ALITALIA
I-SPY points: 10

Date: _____

AUSTRIAN ARROWS
I-SPY points: 20

Date: _____

BRITISH AIRWAYS
I-SPY points: 5

Date: _____

AIR JAMAICA

I-SPY points: 25

Date: _____

**AMERICAN
AIRLINES**

I-SPY points: 5

Date: _____

**BALKAN
HOLIDAYS AIR**

I-SPY points: 20

Date: _____

BULGARIA AIR
I-SPY points: 20

Date: _____

CARIBBEAN AIRLINES
I-SPY points: 20

Date: _____

CATHAY PACIFIC
I-SPY points: 5

Date: _____

CHINA AIRLINES
I-SPY points: 15

Date: _____

CONTINENTAL
I-SPY points: 5

Date: _____

CYPRUS AIR
I-SPY points: 15

Date: _____

BMI

I-SPY points: 10

Date: _____

CROATIA AIR

I-SPY points: 20

Date: _____

DHL

I-SPY points: 15

Date: _____

DELTA
I-SPY points: 10
Date: 2 9 ☉ 7o

EASYJET
I-SPY points: 5
Date: 2-6-☉-13

EL AL
I-SPY points: 15
Date:

EMIRATES
I-SPY points: 5
Date:

EVA AIR
I-SPY points: 25
Date:

FEDEX
I-SPY points: 15
Date:

EGYPTAIR

I-SPY points: 20

Date: _____

ETHIOPIAN

I-SPY points: 20

Date: _____

FIRST CHOICE

I-SPY points: 10

Date: _____

FINNAIR
I-SPY points: 15

Date:

FLYBE
I-SPY points: 10

Date: 26-7-73
29.7.

IBERIA
I-SPY points: 10

Date:

IBERWORLD
I-SPY points: 20

Date:

ICELANDAIR
I-SPY points: 20

Date:

KLM
I-SPY points: 10

Date:

Tail Fins and Identification

HELVETIC

I-SPY points: 20

Date: _____

IRAN AIR

I-SPY points: 20

Date: _____

JAPAN AIRLINES

I-SPY points: 15

Date: _____

KUWAIT
I-SPY points: 20

Date:

LIBYAN ARAB
I-SPY points: 25

Date:

LOT POLAND
I-SPY points: 20

Date:

MALAYSIA AIRLINE
I-SPY points: 20

Date:

MONARCH AIR
I-SPY points: 10

Date: 29 076

MIDDLE EAST AIR
I-SPY points: 15

Date:

KOREAN AIRLINES

I-SPY points: 20

Date: _____

LUFTHANSA

I-SPY points: 10

Date: _____

MY TRAVEL

I-SPY points: 10

Date: _____

OLYMPIC
I-SPY points: 15

Date:

ONE WORLD
I-SPY points: 5

Date:

QATAR
I-SPY points: 10

Date:

QANTAS
I-SPY points: 10

Date:

ROYAL JORDAN
I-SPY points: 15

Date:

RYANAIR
I-SPY points: 5

Date: 29·07·

Tail Fins and Identification

PAKISTAN INTERNATIONAL

I-SPY points: 20

Date: _____

ROYAL BRUNEI

I-SPY points: 20

Date: _____

SRI LANKAN

I-SPY points: 20

Date: _____

SINGAPORE
I-SPY points: 5

Date:

SOUTH AFRICA
I-SPY points: 5

Date:

SWISS
I-SPY points: 10

Date:

TAP AIR PORTUGAL
I-SPY points: 15

Date: 12

US AIRWAYS
I-SPY points: 10

Date:

WIZZ AIR
I-SPY points: 10

Date:

THAI AIRWAYS

I-SPY points: 10

Date: _____

THOMSON

I-SPY points: 10

Date: _____

TRANSAERO RUSSIA

I-SPY points: 25

Date: _____

TURKISH AIR

I-SPY points: 20

Date: _____

UNITED AIRLINES

I-SPY points: 10

Date: _____

VIRGIN ATLANTIC

I-SPY points: 5

Date: 2·7 7-3